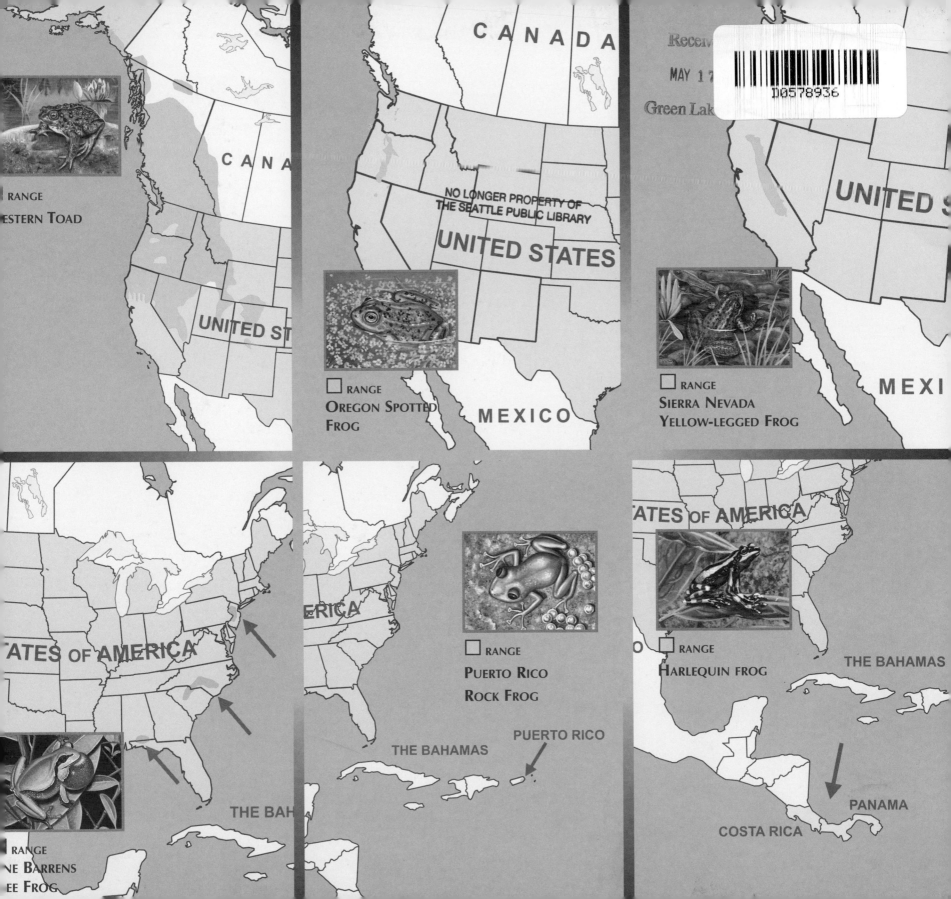

□ RANGE

ESTERN TOAD

UNITED STATES

CANADA

MEXICO

□ RANGE

OREGON SPOTTED
FROG

□ RANGE

SIERRA NEVADA
YELLOW-LEGGED FROG

□ RANGE

NE BARRENS
EE FROG

□ RANGE

PUERTO RICO
ROCK FROG

THE BAHAMAS

PUERTO RICO

□ RANGE

HARLEQUIN FROG

THE BAHAMAS

COSTA RICA

PANAMA

Recei

MAY 1 7

Green Lak

A PLACE FOR
FROGS

For Emile, a fellow frog lover

—M. S.

With sincere gratitude to Anita Grien

—H. B.

Published by
PEACHTREE PUBLISHERS
1700 Chattahoochee Avenue
Atlanta, Georgia 30318-2112

www.peachtree-online.com

Book design by Loraine M. Joyner
Composition by Melanie McMahon Ives
Illustrations created in acrylic on cold press illustration board.
Title typeset in Nick Curtis's HardlyWorthIt; main text typeset in
Monotype's Century Schoolbook with Apple's Techno initial capitals;
sidebar titles typeset in Apple's Techno, and text typeset in Adobe's
Optima.

Printed and manufactured in November 2009 by Imago in Singapore
10 9 8 7 6 5 4 3 2 1
First Edition

Library of Congress Cataloging-in-Publication Data
Stewart, Melissa.
  A place for frogs / written by Melissa Stewart ; illustrated by Higgins
Bond.
      p. cm.
  ISBN 978-1-56145-521-8
  1. Frogs—Habitat—Juvenile literature. 2. Nature—Effect of human
beings on—Juvenile literature. I. Bond, Higgins, ill. II. Title.
  QL668.E2S745 2010
  597.8'9217—dc22
                                              2009024515

A PLACE FOR

FROGS

Written by
Melissa Stewart

Illustrated by
Higgins Bond

Frogs make our world a better place. But sometimes people do things that make it hard for them to live and grow.

If we work together to help these special creatures, there will always be a place for frogs.

A FROG'S LIFE

As frogs grow, they go through four life stages. After mating, a female frog lays eggs in a wet place. When a tiny tadpole breaks out of its egg, it spends most of its time eating and growing. Soon the tadpole begins to develop legs. Its tail shrinks, and it starts breathing air. The froglet hops onto land. It grows quickly and loses its tail. When it becomes a full-grown frog, it is ready to find a mate.

GREEN FROG

For frogs to survive, they need to stay safe and healthy.
Some frogs are harmed by poisons used to kill insects.

CALIFORNIA RED-LEGGED FROG

Because frogs have thin skin, they are very sensitive to human-made chemicals. When people in Northern California sprayed poisons to kill insects that harm crops, many California red-legged frogs died too. In 2006, the Center for Biological Diversity forced people to stop using the chemicals that harm frogs. Now scientists are hoping the frogs can make a comeback.

When people stop spraying these dangerous chemicals, frogs can live and grow.

Some tadpoles are harmed by chemicals farmers use to make crops grow bigger and stronger.

When farmers and scientists find new ways to improve their crops, frogs can live and grow.

Northern Leopard Frog

In 1995, students in Henderson, Minnesota, found frogs with deformed legs at a local pond. It took scientists many years to figure out what was wrong.

When fertilizers from fields drained into the pond, the population of tiny flatworms exploded. The worms burrowed into the tadpoles' bodies and their legs couldn't develop normally. Now that scientists understand the problem, they are searching for a solution.

Some frogs lay their eggs in shallow ponds. The eggs can be damaged by too much sunlight.

WESTERN TOAD

In the 1960s, people began using chemicals called CFCs in refrigerators and air conditioners. As the CFCs rose into the sky, they destroyed the part of Earth's atmosphere that blocks the sun's harmful rays. Super-strong sunlight killed many developing western toad tadpoles before they hatched. In 1995, CFCs were banned. By 2003, Earth's atmosphere had begun to block more sunlight. Scientists hope that it is not too late to save western toads.

When people find ways to block some of the sun's harmful rays, frogs can live and grow.

Some frogs have trouble surviving when people introduce new plants to a natural habitat.

When people grow native plants to feed their horses and cattle,
frogs can live and grow.

OREGON SPOTTED FROG

As Americans moved westward in the 1800s, some of them planted reed canary grass to feed their animals. It grew so thick that Oregon spotted frogs had trouble finding places to lay their eggs. Soon, the frogs were almost gone. Now that scientists know why Oregon spotted frogs are disappearing, they can remove the reed canary grass and replace it with native plants.

ome tadpoles have trouble surviving when people add fish to lakes and ponds.

SIERRA NEVADA YELLOW-LEGGED FROG

Because the lakes high in the Sierra Nevada Mountains are so beautiful, people thought it would be fun to go fishing there. They added tons of trout to the lakes. It didn't take long for the fish to devour most of the yellow-legged tadpoles. When scientists noticed the problem, they convinced people to remove the trout. Then the frog population began to recover.

When people take out the fish, frogs can live and grow.

Frogs have trouble surviving when their natural homes are destroyed.
Many frogs lay their eggs in wetlands that dry up in the summer.

When people protect these part-time ponds, frogs can live and grow.

HOUSTON TOAD

In the 1960s, people started building homes, businesses, and parking lots on the land where Houston toads lived. As workers filled in temporary ponds, Houston toads began to disappear. But now scientists realize how important the pools are. They have asked people to build fences around the pools so Houston toads have a place to lay their eggs. If people protect enough ponds, the toads can make a comeback.

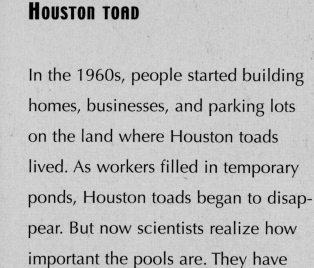

Frogs that lay eggs in part-time ponds live in nearby forests. They travel to the pools each spring to mate and lay eggs. Sometimes they are killed when they try to cross busy roads.

WOOD FROG

Frogs don't know that roads are dangerous, and drivers can't always stop in time. In some towns, people watch for wood frogs on warm, rainy nights in early spring. When they see migrating frogs, the caring citizens stop traffic while the frogs hop across the road.

When people make the trip safer, frogs can live and grow.

Some frogs can only survive in sunny, open woodlands.

GOPHER FROG

At one time, natural wildfires regularly burned back plants in areas where gopher frogs live. But when people settled in the area, they put out the fires. Some plants grew large, crowding out the smaller plants gopher tadpoles depend on for food and shelter. In spring, the big plants sucked up wetland water before tadpoles could develop into frogs. When scientists noticed the problem, they began to carefully burn some forest areas so gopher frogs can survive.

When people work to restore these wild places, frogs can live and grow.

Other frogs depend on wetlands surrounded by thick, low shrubs.

When people work to save these watery worlds, frogs can live and grow.

PINE BARRENS TREE FROG

In the late 1950s, the members of a county planning board in New Jersey proposed cutting down a pineland forest and building an airport. The project would have destroyed dozens of ponds where Pine Barrens tree frogs live. Fortunately, scientists and citizens worked together to stop the project and protect the land forever. Thanks to their efforts, Pine Barrens tree frogs will always have a place to live.

Some frogs can only live in cool, dark, rocky places.

PUERTO RICO ROCK FROG

The Puerto Rico rock frog lives in small caves in the southeastern part of Puerto Rico, an island in the Caribbean Sea. For many years, local people dumped their garbage in the caves. But now the dumping has stopped and citizens are cleaning up the caves. A healthy habitat will help the frogs survive.

When people use less oil, coal, and natural gas to heat their homes and power their cars, it helps slow down global warming. Then frogs can live and grow.

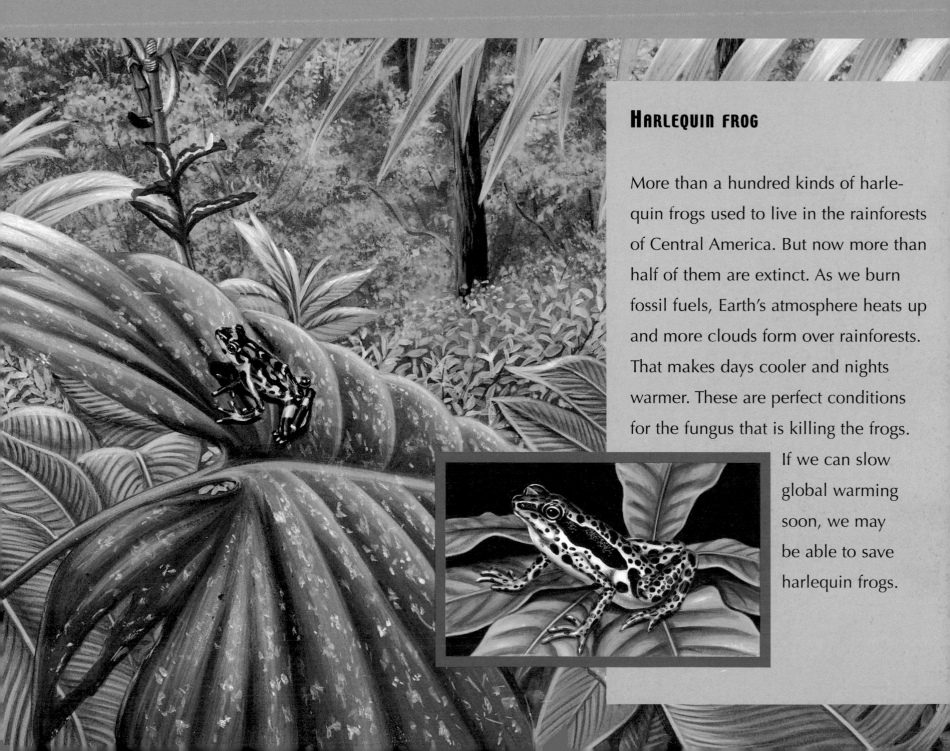

HARLEQUIN FROG

More than a hundred kinds of harlequin frogs used to live in the rainforests of Central America. But now more than half of them are extinct. As we burn fossil fuels, Earth's atmosphere heats up and more clouds form over rainforests. That makes days cooler and nights warmer. These are perfect conditions for the fungus that is killing the frogs.

If we can slow global warming soon, we may be able to save harlequin frogs.

When too many frogs die, other living things may also have trouble surviving.

WE NEED FROGS

Frogs help us survive. By eating insects, frogs protect farmers' crops and help us stay healthy. Frogs are very sensitive to changes in the environment. When we see problems in our frogs, it warns us of dangers that might affect other plants and animals too. Then we can look for ways to fix the problems.

That's why it's so important to protect frogs and the places where they live.

OTHER ANIMALS NEED FROGS

Frogs are an important part of the food chain. Eggs and tadpoles are good sources of food for fish, large water insects, and ducks. Adult frogs are eaten by fish, snakes, lizards, bats, otters, foxes, water shrews, and birds. Without frogs, many other creatures would go hungry.

Frogs have lived on Earth for about 200 million years.

HELPING FROGS

Do not catch and keep frogs. Let them live in their natural environment.

Do not buy frogs at a pet store. Frogs are wild animals and should live in their natural homes.

If someone gives you a frog, do not release it in a wild place. It could eat other frogs or make them sick.

Do not eat frogs' legs. Ask local restaurants not to serve them.

Do not spray chemicals that could harm frogs.

Sometimes people do things that can harm frogs. But there are many ways you can help these special creatures live far into the future.

Join a group of people keeping track of frogs that live in your area.

Join a group of people working to protect or restore wetlands near your home.

Talk to teachers at your school about celebrating Save the Frogs Day. You can get more information about events happening near you at *http://save thefrogs.com/day.*

FASCINATING FROG FACTS

No one knows exactly how many kinds of frogs live on Earth. So far, scientists have discovered and named almost five thousand different species. But people keep on finding new kinds of frogs every year.

The microfrog is the smallest frog on Earth. It's about the size of your fingernail. The Goliath frog is the world's largest frog. It's as big as a rabbit.

About five hundred kinds of frogs belong to a family called the "true toads." They have dry, scaly skin and spend more time on land than other frogs. That means all toads are frogs, but not all frogs are toads.

A female western toad can lay up to 16,500 eggs at a time. But less than 1 percent of those eggs hatch and develop into adults. The lucky few western toads that do grow up may live more than thirty-five years.

Harlequin frog tadpoles can only eat one kind of food—extra eggs laid by their moms.

In winter, wood frogs bury themselves in leaves and freeze solid. In spring, the males attract mates with a call that sounds like a quacking duck.